The Fall of the Roman World and the Rise of Christianity

Power and Religion in Medieval and Renaissance Times

The Fall of the Roman World and the Rise of Christianity

Edited by Kelly Roscoe

Britannica Educational Publishing
in association with
ROSEN
EDUCATIONAL SERVICES

Published in 2018 by Britannica Educational Publishing (a trademark of Encyclopædia Britannica, Inc.) in association with The Rosen Publishing Group, Inc.
29 East 21st Street, New York, NY 10010

Distributed exclusively by Rosen Publishing.
To see additional Britannica Educational Publishing titles, go to rosenpublishing.com.

First Edition

Britannica Educational Publishing
J.E. Luebering: Executive Director, Core Editorial
Andrea R. Field: Managing Editor, Compton's by Britannica

Rosen Publishing
Meredith Day: Editor
Nelson Sá: Art Director
Brian Garvey: Designer
Cindy Reiman: Photography Manager
Bruce Donnola: Photo Researcher

Library of Congress Cataloging-in-Publication Data

Names: Roscoe, Kelly, editor.
Title: The fall of the Roman world and the rise of Christianity / edited by Kelly Roscoe.
Description: First edition. | New York : Britannica Educational Publishing, 2018. | Series: Power and religion i
Medieval and Renaissance times | Includes bibliographical references and index. | Audience: Grade 9 to 12.
Identifiers: LCCN 2016053736 | ISBN 9781680486254 (library bound : alk. paper)
Subjects: LCSH: Rome--History--Empire, 284-476. | Rome--History--Germanic Invasions, 3rd-6th centuries
Church history--Primitive and early church, ca. 30-600.
Classification: LCC DG311 .F34 2017 | DDC 937/.0607204--dc23
LC record available at https://lccn.loc.gov/2016053736

Manufactured in China

Photo credits: Cover pp. 3, 13, 30, 54, 75 Conde/Shutterstock.com; pp. 8-9 SCALA/Art Resource, New York; p. 14 Bibliote Medicea-Laurenziana, Florence, Italy/Bridgeman Images; pp. 18, 69 ullstein bild/Getty Images; pp. 20, 22 Courtesy of the National Portrait Gallery, London; p. 23 Courtesy of the Universitats-Bibliothek Basel; p 26 Manuel Litran/Paris Match Arc Getty Images; p. 28 Universal Images Group/Hulton Fine Art Collection/Getty Images; pp. 32, 44, Encyclopædia Britanni Inc.; pp. 34-35, 39, 41, 84-85 Photos.com/Thinkstock; pp. 36-37 Alvaro German Vilela/Shutterstock.com; p. 50 Universal History Archive/Universal Images Group/Getty Images; pp. 52-53 Universal Images Group/Getty Images; pp. 56-57 De Agostini/S. Vannini/Getty Images; p. 59 Giraudon/Art Resource, New York; p. 61 Bridgeman Images; pp. 62-63 Interfoto/A Stock Photo; pp. 64-65 Alvaro Canovas/Paris Match/Getty Images; p. 67 Print Collector/Hulton Archive/Getty Images; p. Anderson—Alinari/Art Resource, New York; pp. 72-73 Galleria Sabauda, Turin, Italy/Bridgeman Images; p. 76 Heritage Im Hulton Archive/Getty Images; p. 78 Heritage Images/Hulton Fine Art Collection/Getty Images; p. 80 Abbey of Monte Ca Cassino, Italy/Bridgeman Images; p. 82 Huntington Library and Art Gallery, San Marino, CA, USA/Bridgeman Images; p. 8 Madame.evangelista; p. 89 Courtesy of the Staatsbibliothek Bamberg; p. 90 Kunsthistorisches Museum, Vienna; interior pa background and border graphics Roberto Castillo/Shutterstock.com; back cover flourish Drakonova/Shutterstock.com

Contents

Introduction

The medieval period, or the Middle Ages, was a time in European history before the modern era. In the 4th century CE Germanic peoples began crossing the frontiers of the Roman Empire, in part because of the advance of ferocious warriors from the east—the Huns. The movement of the Germanic peoples contributed to the so-called fall of the Roman Empire. Although violent clashes occurred between the Romans and various Germanic tribes, the process also involved the more peaceful migration and settlement of Germanic peoples in the empire and their incorporation in Roman armies. The Germanic peoples themselves underwent important social and cultural changes as a result of their contact with Rome. They were gradually "Romanized," adopting various Roman traditions—including Christianity—and they became more settled. The union of Germanic traditions and Roman religion and culture led to the emergence of the civilization of the Middle Ages.

Even before the fall of the Western Roman Empire in 476, life in Europe began to change. The Germanic peoples had long lived along the frontiers of the Roman Empire. In the 3rd century, during a period of near-anarchy within the empire, they attempted to seize Roman territory. The Roman recovery of the late 3rd and 4th centuries restored the traditional balance. At the same time, the Romans began to welcome some of these people into the empire. Some were

This 5th-century mosaic in the church of Santa Maria Maggiore in Rome depicts the crossing of the Red Sea.

settled inside the Roman lines as farmers and defenders of the frontier, and others were recruited for the Roman army. The Germanic peoples in this way became part of the empire and learned Roman ways. In the later 4th century, however, this balance was upset by the appearance of another people, the Huns.

The Huns began moving westward from their homeland north of China in the 4th century, conquering everyone in their way and inspiring great fear. They achieved their greatest success in the 5th century under their leader Attila. As a result of the savage advance of the Huns, the Germanic peoples along the frontier began moving into Roman territory. This movement of the Germanic tribes has traditionally been called the barbarian invasions, since the Romans called foreigners from outside the empire "barbarians."

The Romans themselves settled some of these Germanic peoples within the empire, while others invaded and conquered Roman territory. The arrival of the Germanic peoples occurred at a time, especially in the Western Empire, when Rome suffered economic and population declines that made it less able to turn back the invaders. From the 4th to 6th centuries Goths, Vandals, Lombards, Franks, Angles, Saxons, and other Germanic tribes entered the empire and created new kingdoms on the ruins of the old Roman world.

The early medieval period has sometimes been called the late antique period or the Dark Ages because it was believed to have been a time of violence and ignorance. This view has generally been rejected, however, and many historians now regard it as a time of significant transformation from one form of civilization to another. In fact, many changes took place during this period that laid important foundations for later developments. The Germanic peoples who settled in the empire did not possess the highly developed systems of law and government of the Romans. However, they followed long-standing customs that served as legal traditions and were organized in war bands led by warrior chiefs. These chiefs, partly as a result of contact with Rome, evolved into powerful kings. The Germanic peoples adopted, if in simpler form, Roman administrative traditions, especially in the area of taxation. The new Germanic rulers also inherited the language of government and the practice of writing and codifying the law from the Romans.

The creation of new kingdoms out of the old Roman state yielded some dynamic cultures, especially those of the Ostrogoths (eastern Goths) of Italy and the Visigoths (western Goths) of Spain. Although the Germanic peoples enveloped Europe and drove into North Africa, only one group, the Franks, created a lasting state. Their first great leader was Clovis, who in 481–511 established in Gaul the kingdom that was to become France.

Clovis not only set the foundation for a long-lasting kingdom, but he also converted to Christianity, probably in 496 but possibly later. Many Germanic peoples had become Christians earlier. Most of them had adopted the Arian doctrine, however, which was condemned as heresy (a doctrine contrary to church teachings) by the Roman Catholic

Church. Clovis was one of the first of the Germanic kings to convert to Roman Catholic Christianity, and with him the entire kingdom accepted the faith.

When Clovis became a Roman Catholic, his Franks began to receive the support of the bishops and other religious figures in his kingdom. This opened to the Franks the residue of Roman culture sustained by the church. Its monks, living in retreats called monasteries, had preserved a knowledge of Roman arts, crafts, and industries. The monasteries were also important centres of book production and education, and they now began to spread this learning.

Chapter One

The Idea of the Middle Ages

Many historians have questioned the conventional dating of the beginning and end of the Middle Ages, which were never precise and cannot be located in any year or even century. Some scholars have advocated extending the period defined as late antiquity (*c.* 250–*c.* 750 CE) into the 10th century or later, and some have proposed a Middle Ages lasting from about 1000 to 1800. Still others argue for the inclusion of the old periods Middle Ages, Renaissance, and Reformation into a single period beginning in late antiquity and ending in the late 16th century.

Historiography Before the 18th Century

From the 4th to the 15th century, writers of history thought within a linear framework of time derived from the Chris-

St. Augustine, seen here preaching to his disciples, adapted classical thought to Christian teaching and created a theological system of great power and lasting influence.

tian understanding of Scripture—the sequence of Creation, Incarnation, Christ's Second Coming, and the Last Judgment. In Book XXII of *City of God*, the great Church Father Augustine of Hippo (354–430) posited six ages of world history, which paralleled the six days of Creation and the six ages of the individual human life span. For Augustine, the six ages of history—from Adam and Eve to the Flood, from the Flood to Abraham, from Abraham to King David, from David to the Babylonian Exile, from the Exile to Jesus Christ, and from Christ to the Second Coming—would be followed by a seventh age, the reign of Christ on earth. World history was conceived as "salvation history"—the course of events from Creation to the Last Judgment—and its purposes were religious and moral. Thus, all the references by Augustine and other early authors to a "middle time" must be understood within the framework of the sixth age of salvation history.

Early Christian interpretations of the biblical Book of Daniel (Daniel 2:31–45, 7), especially those of the Church Father Jerome (c. 347–419/420) and the historian Paulus Orosius (flourished 414–417), added the idea of four successive world empires—Babylon, Persia, Greece, and Rome. Late writers in this tradition added the idea of the *translatio imperii* ("translation of empire"): from Alexander the Great to the Romans, from the Romans to the Franks under Charlemagne in 800, and from Charlemagne to the East Frankish emperors and Otto I. A number of early European thinkers built upon the idea of the translation of empire to define European civilization in terms of scholarship and chivalry (the knightly code of conduct). All these ideas were readily compatible with the Augustinian sequence of the six ages of the world.

DIVIDING UP TIME

The 8th-century English monk and computist Bede (673–735), adapting an invention of the 6th-century theologian Dionysius Exiguus, introduced the method of counting years from the birth of Jesus, *anno Domini* ("in the year of our Lord"), which formed the basis of the modern notion of the Common Era. The new method superseded older traditions, which included dating by four-year Olympiads, by the number of years since the founding of Rome in 753 BCE, by the years of Roman consuls, by the regnal years of emperors, and by the 15-year assessment cycle of indictions. Bede's innovation was taken up by Frankish chroniclers and rulers from the late 8th century and became standard practice in Europe.

The year itself was divided according to a universal Christian calendar that gradually displaced the old Roman calendar, although it retained the Roman names for the months. The liturgical year alternated seasons of penitence and joy, beginning with Advent, the fifth Sunday before Christmas, and culminating in penitential Lent and joyful Easter and its aftermath until Advent returned. Although the unit of the week and the Sabbath were taken over from Jewish usage—displacing the older Roman divisions of the month into Kalendae, Nonae, and Ides and the nine-day market cycle—Christians began to mark time by the seven-day week and moved its holiest day to Sunday during the 4th century.

The single exception to this trend was the work of the late 12th-century Calabrian abbot and scriptural exegete Joachim of Fiore (c. 1130–c. 1201). According to Joachim, there were three ages in human history: that of the Father (before Christ), that of the Son (from Christ to an unknown future date, which some of Joachim's followers located in the late 13th century), and that of the Holy Spirit (during which all Christendom would turn into a vast church with a universal priesthood of believers). But Joachim's view was also firmly expressed in terms of salvation history. Many chroniclers and writers of histories, of course, wrote about shorter periods of time and focused their efforts on local affairs, but the great Augustinian metanarrative underlay their work too. From several confessional perspectives, this view still survives.

In the 14th century, however, the literary moralist Petrarch (1304–74), fascinated with ancient Roman history and contemptuous of the time that followed it, including his own century, divided the past into ancient and new—antiquity and recent times—and located the transition between them in the 4th century, when the Roman emperors converted to Christianity. According to Petrarch, what followed was an age of *tenebrae* ("shadows"), a "sordid middle time" with only the hope of a better age to follow. Although Petrarch's disapproval of the Christianized Roman and post-Roman world may seem irreligious, he was in fact a devout Christian. His judgment was based on aesthetic, moral, and philological criteria, not Christian ones. Petrarch's limitless admiration for Rome heralded a novel conception of the European past and established criteria for historical periodization other than those of salvation history or the history of the church, empire, cities, rulers, or noble dynasties. His followers in later centuries focused primarily on the transformation of the arts and letters, seeing a renewal of earlier Roman dignity and achievement beginning with the painter Giotto (1266/67 or 1276–1337) and with Petrarch himself and continuing into the 15th and 16th centuries.

Petrarch was regarded as the greatest scholar of his age. The hallmark of his thought was a deep consciousness of the past as the nutriment of the present.

In the early 16th century, religious critics and reformers, including both the Dutch humanist Desiderius Erasmus and the Protestant reformer Martin Luther, added another dimension to the new conception and terminology: the idea of an evangelical, apostolic Christian church that had become corrupt when it was absorbed by the Roman Empire and now needed to be reformed, or restored to its earlier apostolic authenticity. The idea of reform had long been built into the Christian worldview. This conception of the period between the 4th and 16th centuries was laid out in the great Protestant history by Matthias Flacius Illyricus, *Centuriae Magdeburgensis* (1559–74; "The Magdeburg Centuries"), which also introduced the practice of dividing the past into ostensibly neutral centuries. The Roman Catholic version of church history was reflected in the *Annales Ecclesiastici* ("Ecclesiastical Annals") of Caesar Baronius (1538–1607), completed by Oderico Rinaldi in 1677. Thus, the historical dimension of both the Protestant and the Catholic reformations of the 16th and 17th centuries added a sharply controversial religious interpretation of the Christian past to Petrarch's original conception, as church history was put to the service of confessional debate.

Petrarch's cultural successors, the literary humanists, also used variants of the expression "Middle Ages." Among them was *media tempestas* ("middle time"), first used by Giovanni Andrea, bishop of Aleria, in 1469; others were *media antiquitas* ("middle antiquity"), *media aetas* ("middle era"), and *media tempora* ("middle times"), all first used between 1514 and 1530. The political theorist and historian Melchior Goldast appears to have coined the variation *medium aevum* ("a middle age") in 1604. Shortly after, in a Latin work of 1610, the

John Selden was a legal antiquarian, Orientalist, and politician who was the leading figure in the Antiquarian Society, the centre of English historical research during the 17th century.

English jurist and legal historian John Selden repeated *medium aevum*, Anglicizing the term in 1614 to "middle times" and in 1618 to "middle ages." In 1641 the French historian Pierre de Marca apparently coined the French vernacular term *le moyen âge*, which gained authority in the respected lexicographical work *Glossarium ad scriptores mediae et infimae latinitatis* (1678; "A Glossary for Writers of Middle and Low Latin"), by Charles du Fresne, seigneur du Cange, who emphasized the inferior and "middle" quality of Latin linguistic usage after the 4th century. Other 17th-century historians, including Gisbertus Voetius and Georg Horn, used terms such as *media aetas* in their histories of the church before the Reformation of the 16th century.

The term and idea circulated even more widely in other historical works. Du Cange's great dictionary also used the Latin term *medium aevum*, as did the popular historical textbook *The Nucleus of Middle History Between Ancient and Modern* (1688), by the German historian Christoph Keller—although Keller observed that in naming the period he was simply following the terminology of earlier and contemporary scholars. By the late 17th century the most commonly used term for the period in Latin was *medium aevum*, and various equivalents of Middle Ages or Middle Age were used in European vernacular languages.

ENLIGHTENMENT SCORN AND ROMANTIC ADMIRATION

During the 17th and 18th centuries a number of thinkers argued that western Europe after the 15th century had surpassed even antiquity in its discoveries and technology and had thereby created a distinctively modern world. Their views, which were sharpened by Enlightenment critics of earlier European political and religious structures, did nothing to change the image of the Middle Ages. Voltaire, in his *An Essay on Universal History, the Manners and Spirit of Nations from the Reign of Charlemaign to the Age of Lewis XIV* (1756), savaged the Latin Christian and the reformed churches for their clerical obscurantism and earlier rulers for their ruthless and arbitrary use of force. Edward Gibbon, the English historian whose great work *The Decline and Fall of the Roman Empire* (1776–88) begins with events in late antiquity and ends with the fall of Constantinople (the capital of the Byzantine Empire) to the Ottoman Turks in 1453, categorically attributed the beginning of that very long "decline and fall" to "the triumph of barbarism and religion," thus contemptuously characterizing the entire period from the 5th to the 15th century.

But, as Gibbon's own work showed, not only had the term and the often pejorative idea of the Middle Ages been

This oil painting of Edward Gibbon by Henry Walton in 1774 hangs in the National Portrait Gallery in London.

shaped in the 16th and 17th centuries, but so had the critical and technical standards of modern historical scholarship. Some Enlightenment thinkers even became interested in earlier periods of European history. Their attraction to the Middle Ages paralleled the respect for and interest in the period shared by many ideologically conservative rulers, nobles, magistrates, and churchmen. But the historians also began to apply critical techniques to their investigation of the Middle Ages. The new scholarship on the period was animated in the late 18th and early 19th centuries by historians imbued with ethnic-national sentiment and with a conception of historically "ethnic" communities—especially in Germany and England—that lacked a recognized past (or had only a peripheral past) in traditional histories of the Greco-Roman world.

During the Romantic era, an affectionate and sentimentalized portrait of the Middle Ages emerged that was usually no more accurate than the controversial characterizations of Enlightenment writers. Such views contributed to the myth that 19th-century nation-states were composed of ethnic groups that had remained unchanged and had occupied the same territory for long periods (or had once occupied territory that was now inhabited by other nation-states). These arguments became powerful and dangerous political forces in the 19th and 20th centuries, although research in the late 20th century dismissed them as political fantasies.

Not all 19th-century historians were appreciative of the Middle Ages. Although the French historian Jules Michelet at first praised the Middle Ages as the time of the birth of France, his increasing political liberalism led him to shift his admiration to the 16th century, virtually coining the term "Renaissance" in the process of appropriating it for France. In 1860 Swiss historian Jacob Burckhardt published his *The Civilization of the Renaissance in Italy*, a work as widely read and influential as that of Michelet. Despite Romantic nostalgia and increasingly disciplined scholarship, the work of Michelet and Burckhardt served to fix the opposi-

Jacob Burckhardt, seen here in 1892, was one of the first great historians of art and culture.

tion between the Middle Ages and the Renaissance in the modern mind, generally to the disadvantage of the former. These views were sharpened by 19th-century anticlericalism, especially anti-Roman Catholicism, although they were countered by equally learned Catholic apologists.

The Middle Ages in Modern Historiography

With the extraordinary growth of the academic discipline of history in the 19th century, the history of the Middle Ages was absorbed into academic curricula of history in Europe and the United States and established in university survey courses and research seminars. Journals of scholarly historical research began publication in Germany (1859), France (1876), England (1886), and the United States (1895), regularly including studies of one aspect or another of the Middle Ages. Historical documents were edited and substantial scholarly literature was produced that brought the history of the Middle Ages into synchronization with other fields of history. The study of the Middle Ages developed chiefly as a part of the national histories of the individual European countries, but it was studied in the United States as a pan-European phenomenon, with a focus after World War I chiefly on English and French history. The growing influence and prestige of the new academic and professional field of medieval history were reflected in the Monumenta Germaniae Historica ("Historical Monuments of the Germans"), a research and publication institute founded in 1819 and still in operation in Munich, and in the eight-volume collaborative *Cambridge Medieval History* (1911–36). (The latter's replacement, *The New Cambridge Medieval History,* began to appear in 1998.)

Most scholars of the 19th and early 20th centuries accepted the view that history is largely a story of progress, in which occasional periods of decline—such as the Middle Ages—are succeeded by periods of renewal. The most articulate attack on this view was by the American medievalist Charles Homer Haskins in *The Renaissance of the Twelfth Century* (1927), which applied Michelet's and Burckhardt's term "Renaissance" to the 12th century rather than to the 15th or 16th.

Although the teaching responsibilities of academic historians of the Middle Ages still generally reflect either the original three-part division of European history or the more recent and more common four-part division (ancient, medieval, early modern, and modern), most scholars specialize in only very small parts of a very long period. With the emergence of late antiquity as a distinct field of research and teaching since the mid-20th century, the early part of the conventional Middle Ages has been rethought and rewritten. The distinctive post-Classical period of late antiquity is now considered the medium through which ancient Greco-Roman traditions were passed on to later Europeans. The older image of a Classical antiquity despised by world-rejecting Christians and wiped out by savage barbarians is no longer credible.

Historians in the late 20th and early 21st centuries also debated the existence of a rapid and extensive change in European society at about the turn of the 2nd millennium. Some scholars, following the pioneering lead of the French historian Georges Duby, argued for a rapid mutation, chiefly with regard to the development of new kinds

Georges Duby (1919–1996) was one of the 20th century's most prolific and influential historians of the Middle Ages.

of lay and ecclesiastical power over agricultural labour and the simultaneous restructuring of aristocratic lineages in the 11th century. Others maintained that a gradual transformation of society and culture occurred over a longer period of time, beginning earlier than the 11th century. These debates influenced the concept of a long Middle Ages mentioned above.

With the emergence of the concept of early modern history, roughly from 1400 to 1800, the Middle Ages, the Renaissance, the Reformation, and the scientific revolution were incorporated into a period extending from the late 14th century to the 18th century. The creation of specialized scholarly conferences, historical journals, monograph series, and thematic collections of scholarly essays has reflected these changes in the configuration of the period.

Scholars also rethought the nature of change in different parts of Europe. They recognized the problem of the obvious differences between those European lands in late antiquity that had once been part of the Roman Empire and those that had not and therefore got their Romanism and antiquity secondhand. They also revised their understanding of the relations between the older Mediterranean world (large areas of which entered the Byzantine and Arab-Islamic cultural orbits) and northern Europe. In addition, scholars examined how Roman culture exported itself to peripheries on the north and east through a form of colonization that culminated in the absorption of originally peripheral colonies into an expanded core culture.

"Middle Ages" remains both a commonplace colloquial term and the name of a subject of academic study. But the history of the term and the current debate about its temporal and spatial application and appropriateness is a reminder that historical periods are cultural and social constructs based on later perceptions of the past. Furthermore, human life often changes quite rapidly within labeled periods, however designated, and the dialogue between continuity and change is the historian's primary intellectual activity.

Regardless of the loaded aesthetic, philological, moral, confessional, and philosophical origins of the term "Middle Ages," the period it defines is important because it witnessed the emergence of a distinctive European civilization centred in a region that was on the periphery of ancient Mediterranean civilization. Although European civilization

This illustration from the 14th-century *Medieval Health Handbook* shows farmers in a banana plantation. Agricultural scenes such as these are iconic imagery from the Middle Ages.

appropriated elements of both Greco-Roman antiquity and Judeo-Christian religion and ethics, it emerged just as the ancient Mediterranean ecumenical world was divided into the civilizations of East Rome, or Byzantium, and Islam in the 7th and 8th centuries. Three sibling civilizations, two of them Christian, developed at about the same time. The influence of wider Eurasian and North African history on that of Europe has attracted the attention of increasing numbers of historians since the late 20th century. But such change does not occur in a single year and not even in a single century. To assign any but an approximate date to the beginning of the end of the Middle Ages, as was once the fashion, is pointless. Far more important is the assessment of the nature of change in different areas of life in different periods and different places between the 3rd and the 16th centuries.

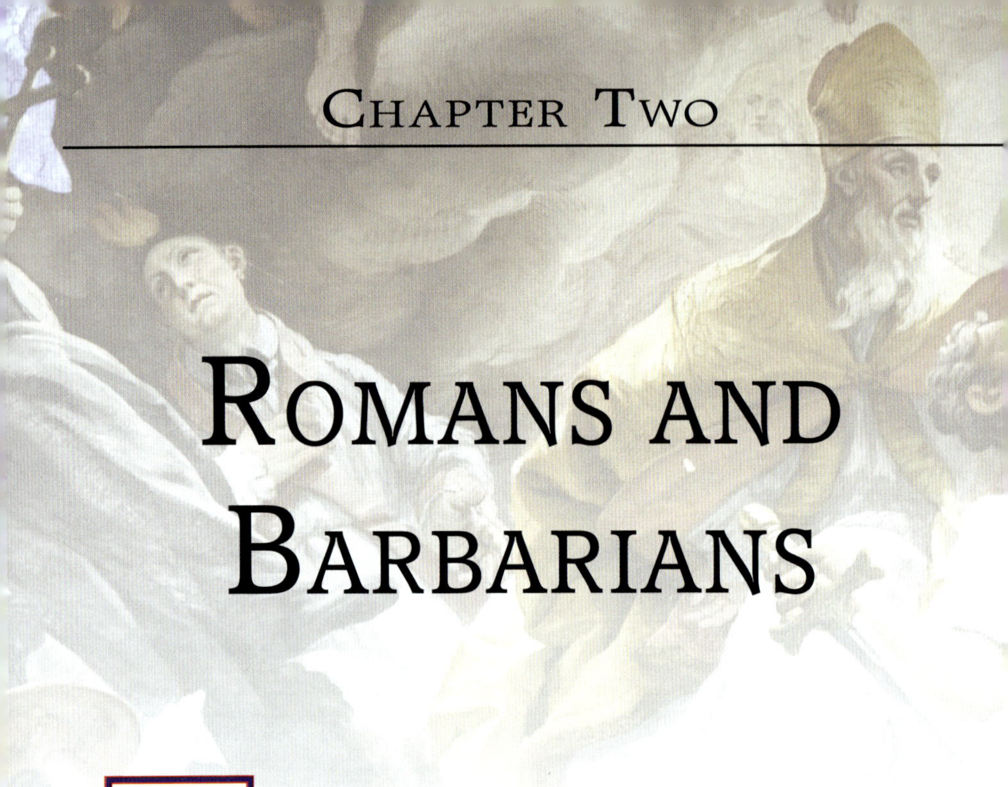

Chapter Two

Romans and Barbarians

The fall of the Western Roman Empire in 476 is generally considered to be the beginning of the Middle Ages. Various Germanic tribes had begun to invade the Roman Empire in the 4th century CE, and they gradually began to adopt the settled lifestyle and Christian traditions of the Roman Empire.

The Romans

The original Mediterranean population of Italy was completely altered by repeated superimpositions of peoples of Indo-European stock. The first Indo-European migrants, who belonged to the Italic tribes, moved across the eastern Alpine passes into the plain of the Po River in about 1800 BCE. Later they crossed the Apennines and eventually occupied the region of Latium, which included Rome. Before 1000

BCE there followed related tribes, which later divided into various groups and gradually moved to central and southern Italy. In Tuscany they were repulsed by the Etruscans, who may have come originally from Anatolia. The next to arrive were Illyrians from the Balkans, who occupied Venetia and Apulia. At the beginning of the historical period, Greek colonists arrived in Italy, and after 400 BCE the Celts, who settled in the plain of the Po.

The city of Rome, increasing gradually in power and influence, created through political rule and the spread of the Latin language something like a nation out of this abundance of nationalities. In this the Romans were favoured by their kinship with the other Italic tribes. The Roman and Italic elements in Italy, moreover, were reinforced in the beginning through the founding of colonies by Rome and by other towns in Latium. The Italic element in Roman towns decreased: a process—less racial than cultural—called the Romanization of the provinces. In the 3rd century BCE, central and southern Italy were dotted with Roman colonies, and the system was to be extended to ever more distant regions up to imperial times. As its dominion spread throughout Italy and covered the entire Mediterranean basin, Rome received an influx of people of the most varied origins, including eventually vast numbers from Asia and Africa.

The building of an enormous empire was Rome's greatest achievement. Held together by the military power of one city, in the 2nd century CE the Roman Empire extended throughout northern Africa and western Asia; in Europe it covered all the Mediterranean countries, Spain, Gaul, and southern Britain. This vast region, united under a single authority and a single political and social organization, enjoyed a long

The Roman Empire in the second century CE extended around the Mediterranean Sea.

period of peaceful development. In Asia, on a narrow front, it bordered the Parthian empire, but elsewhere beyond its perimeter there were only barbarians. Rome brought to the conquered parts of Europe the civilization the Greeks had begun, to which it added its own important contributions in the form of state organization, military institutions, and law. Within the framework of the empire and under the protection of its chain of fortifications, extending uninterrupted the entire length of its frontiers (marked in Europe by the Rhine and the Danube), there began the assimilation of varying types of culture to the Hellenistic-Roman pattern. The army principally, but also Roman administration, the social order, and economic factors, encouraged Romanization. Except around the eastern Mediterranean, where Greek remained dominant, Latin became everywhere the language of commerce and eventually almost the universal language.

The empire formed an interconnected area of free trade, which was afforded a thriving existence by the *pax romana* ("Roman peace"). Products of rural districts found a market throughout the whole empire, and the advanced technical skills of the central region of the Mediterranean spread outward into the provinces. The most decisive step toward Romanization was the extension of the city system into these provinces. Rural and tribal institutions were replaced by the *civitas* form of government, according to which the elected city authority shared in the administration of the surrounding country region. As the old idea of the Greek city-state gained ground, a measure of local autonomy appeared. The Romanized upper classes of the provinces began supplying men to fill the higher offices of the state. Ever-larger numbers of people acquired the status of Roman citizens, until in 212 CE the emperor Caracalla bestowed it on all freeborn subjects. The institution of slavery, however, remained.

The enjoyment of equal rights by all Roman citizens did not last. The population was divided anew into hereditary classes according to their work; and the barbarians, mainly Germanic, who were admitted into the empire in greater numbers, remained in their own tribal associations either as subjects or as allies. The state created a perfected administrative apparatus, which exercised a strongly unifying effect throughout the empire, but local self-government became less and less effective under pressure from the central authority.

An ancient Roman mosaic depicts slaves at work. Roman slave society ended as the slaves were legally converted into *coloni*, or serfs.

The decline of the late empire was accompanied by a stagnation of spiritual forces, a paralysis of creative power, and a retrograde development in the economy. Much of the empire's work of civilization was lost in internal and external wars. Equally, barbarization began with the rise of unchecked pagan ways of life and the settlement of Germanic tribes long before the latter shattered the Western Empire and took possession of its parts. Though many features of Roman civilization disappeared, others survived in the customs of peoples in various parts of the empire. Moreover, something of the superstructure of the empire was taken over by the Germanic states, and much valuable literature was preserved in manuscript for later times.

It was under the Roman Empire that the Christian religion penetrated into Europe. By winning recognition as the religion of the state, it added a new basic factor of equality and unification to the imperial civilization and at the same time reintroduced Middle Eastern and Hellenistic elements into the West. Organized within the framework of the empire, the church became a complementary body upholding the state. Moreover, during the period of the decline of secular culture, Christianity and the church were the sole forces to arouse fresh creative strength by assimilating the civilization of the ancient world and transmitting it to the Middle Ages. At the same time, the church in the West showed reserve

The Basilica of Sant'Apollinare Nuovo in Ravenna, Italy, begun in 535 and consecrated in 549, has impressive capitals in its nave, depicted here, and a distinctive round campanile.

toward the speculative dogma of the Middle Eastern and Hellenic worlds and directed its attention more toward questions of morality and order. When the Western Empire collapsed and the use of Greek had died there, the division between East and West became still sharper. The name Romaioi remained attached to the Greeks of the Eastern Empire, while in the West the word "Roman" developed a new meaning in connection with the church and the bishop of Rome. Christianity and a church of a Roman character, the most enduring legacy of the ancient world, became one of the most important features in western European civilization.

THE GERMANS AND HUNS

The wanderings of the Germanic peoples, which lasted until the early Middle Ages and destroyed the Western Roman Empire, were, together with the migrations of the Slavs, formative elements of the distribution of peoples in modern Europe. The Germanic peoples originated about 1800 BCE from the superimposition, on a population of megalithic culture on the eastern North Sea coast, of Battle-Ax people from the Corded Ware Culture of middle Germany. During the Bronze Age the Germanic peoples spread over southern Scandinavia and penetrated more deeply into Germany between the Weser and Vistula rivers. Contact with the Mediterranean through the amber trade encouraged the development from a purely peasant culture, but during the Iron Age the Germanic peoples were at first cut off from the Mediterranean by the Celts and Illyrians. Their culture declined, and an increasing population, together with worsening climatic conditions, drove them to seek new lands farther south. Thus, the central European Celts and Illyrians found themselves under a growing pressure. Even before 200 BCE the first Germanic tribes had reached the lower Danube, where their path was barred by the Macedonian kingdom. Driven by rising floodwaters, at the end of the 2nd century BCE, migratory hordes of Cimbri, Teutoni, and Ambrones from Jutland broke through the Celtic-Illyrian zone and reached the edge of the Roman sphere of influence, appearing first in Carinthia (113 BCE), then in southern France, and finally in upper Italy.

These migrations were in no way nomadic; they were the gradual expansions of a land-hungry peasantry. Tribes did

This marble bust of Julius Caesar is displayed in the Vatican Museums.

not always migrate en masse. Usually, because of the loose political structure, groups remained in the original homelands or settled down at points along the migration route. In the course of time, many tribes were depleted and scattered. On the other hand, different tribal groups would sometimes unite before migrating or would take up other wanderers en route. The migrations required skilled leadership, and this promoted the social and political elevation of a noble and kingly class.

In 102 BCE the Teutoni were totally defeated by the Romans, who in the following year destroyed the army of the Cimbri. The Swabian tribes, however, moved steadily through central and southern Germany, and the Celts were compelled to retreat to Gaul. When the Germans under Ariovistus crossed the upper Rhine, Julius Caesar arrested their advance and initiated the Roman countermovement with his victory in the Sundgau (58 BCE). Under the emperor Augustus, Roman rule was carried as far as the Rhine and the Danube. On the far side of these rivers, the Germans were pushed back only in the small area contained within the Germano-Raetian *limes* (fortified frontier) from about 70 CE.

The pressure of population was soon evident once more among the German peoples. Tribes that had left Scandinavia earlier (Rugii, Goths, Gepidae, Vandals, Burgundians, and others) pressed on from the lower Vistula and Oder rivers (150 CE onward). The unrest spread to other tribes, and the resulting wars between the Romans and the Marcomanni (166–180) threatened Italy itself. The successful campaigns of Marcus Aurelius resulted in the acquisition by Rome of the provinces of Marcomannia and Sarmatia, but after his death these had to be abandoned and the movement of the

Germanic peoples continued. Soon the Alemanni, pushing up the Main River, reached the upper German limes.

To the east the Goths had reached the Black Sea about 200 CE. Year after year Goths and others, either crossing

Diocletian, Roman emperor from 284 to 305 CE, restored efficient government to the empire after the near anarchy of the 3rd century.

the lower Danube or traveling by sea, penetrated into the Balkan Peninsula and Anatolia as far as Cyprus on plundering expeditions. Only with the Roman victory at Naissus (269) was their advance finally checked. Enriched with booty and constituted imperial mercenaries in return for the payment of a yearly tribute, they became a settled population. The Romans, however, surrendered Dacia beyond the Danube.

In 258 the Alemanni and the Franks broke through the lines and settled on the right bank of the Rhine, continuously infiltrating thereafter toward Gaul and Italy. Everywhere within the empire, towns were fortified, even Rome itself. Franks and Saxons ravaged the coasts of northern Gaul and Britain, and for the next three centuries incursions by Germanic peoples were the scourge of the Western Empire. Nevertheless, it was only with German help that the empire was able to survive as long as it did. The Roman army received an ever-growing number of recruits from the German tribes, which also provided settlers for the land. The Germans soon proved themselves capable of holding the highest ranks in the army. Tribute money to the tribes, pay to individual soldiers, and booty all brought wealth to the Germans, which

CONSTANTINE THE GREAT

Flavius Valerius Constantinus was born in the Roman province of Moesia (later Serbia) about 280 CE. His father, Constantius, was a member of an important Roman family. His mother, Helena, was the daughter of an innkeeper. In 293 the emperor Diocletian made Constantius *caesar*, or emperor, of Gaul and Britain. Young Constantine was kept at the court of Galerius, the Eastern emperor, virtually as a hostage. He escaped in 305 and joined his father. Constantius died the next year, and the army hailed Constantine as caesar.

For five years Constantine was contented with ruling Gaul. Then he invaded Italy, making straight for Rome. Maxentius, the emperor of Rome, came out of the city with his army and met Constantine at the Milvian Bridge. Constantine swept the enemy into the Tiber River, and Maxentius was drowned. Constantine entered Rome as sole master of the Western half of the empire. In 313 he issued the Edict of Milan, which gave the Christians the right to practice their religion openly.

By 323 Constantine had brought the entire Roman world under his own rule. At that time a quarrel threatened to split the Christian church into two camps. Arius, a priest of Alexandria, Egypt, maintained that Christ was not the equal of the Father but was created by Him. Athanasius, leader of the bishops in the West, claimed that the Father and Son, though distinct, were equal, and of the same substance. To settle the matter, Constantine called together an ecumenical, or worldwide, council of bishops at Nicaea, in Asia Minor, in 325. He himself ran the meeting. An overwhelming majority condemned the Arian view as heresy. The Council drew up the Nicene Creed, which is still accepted as the basic doctrine of most Christian churches.

Constantine next moved his seat of government from Rome to the East. For his capital he chose the ancient Greek city of Byzantium on the Bosporus. He enlarged and enriched the city at enormous expense. In 330 it was dedicated as New Rome, but it was generally called Constantinople, "the city of Constantine." The Eastern Roman, or Byzantine, Empire, with its capital at Constantinople (now Istanbul) survived for more than 1,000 years. The new city also became the capital of Christianity in the East, while Rome dominated the religion in the West.

in turn gave warrior lords the means with which to maintain large followings of retainers.

In the West, however, among the Alemanni and Franks, the beginnings of political union into larger groups did not go beyond loose associations. Only in the East did the Gothic kingdom gather many tribes under a single leadership. Above

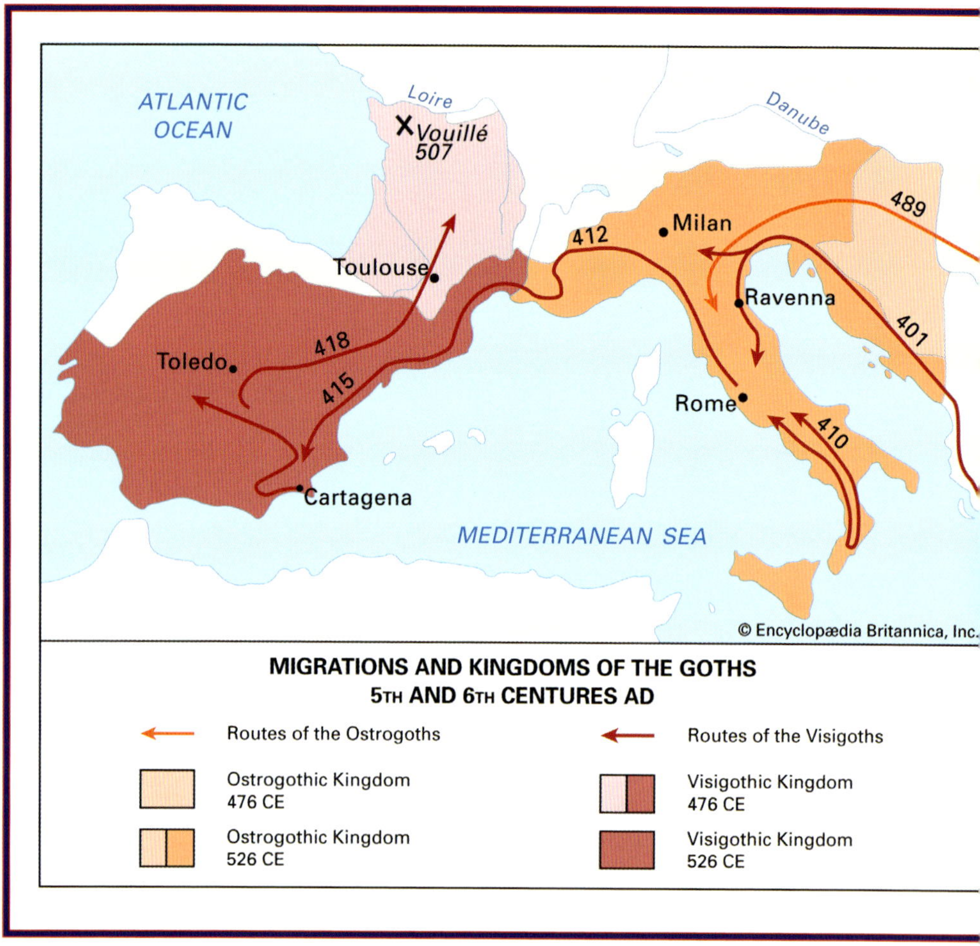

The Franks defeated the Visigoths in 507 at the battle of Vouille (now in France). The Byzantine Empire defeated the Ostrogoths in the mid-500s.

all, the development of the eastern Germans was stimulated by their undisturbed contact with the frontiers of the ancient world. Their economy, however, was still unable to support the needs of a steadily growing population, and pressure from overpopulation resulted in further incursions into the Roman Empire. The imperial reforms of Diocletian and Constantine the Great brought a period of improvement. The usurpation of the imperial title by a Frankish general in 356 let loose a storm along the length of the Rhine and subsequently on the Danube, but the frontiers were restored by the forces of the emperors Julian and Valentinian I, who repelled attacks by both the Franks and the Alemanni.

At that time, a new force appeared. In 375 the Huns from Central Asia first attacked the Ostrogoths—an event that provoked serious disturbances among the eastern Germans. The Huns remained in the background, gradually subjugating many Germanic and other tribes. The terrified Goths and related tribes burst through the Danube frontier into the Roman Empire, and the Balkans became once again a battlefield for German armies. After the crushing defeat of the Romans at Adrianople (378), the empire was no longer in a position to drive all its enemies from its territories. Tribes that could no longer be expelled were settled within the empire as "allies" (*foederati*). They received subsidies and in return supplied troops. The Germanization of the empire progressed, that of the army being nearly completed. None of the tribes, however, that had broken into the Balkans settled there. After the division of the empire in 395, the emperors at Constantinople did all in their power to drive the Germanic tribes away from the vicinity of the capital toward the Western Empire.

In this early 20th-century illustration, Ulfilas teaches Christianity to a group of Goths.

From the beginning of the 5th century, the Western Empire was the scene of numerous further migrations. The Visigoths broke out of the Balkans into Italy and in 410 temporarily occupied Rome. In 406–407, Germanic and other tribes (Vandals, Alani, Suebi, and Burgundians) from Silesia and even farther east crossed the Rhine in their flight from the Huns and penetrated as far as Spain. The Vandals subsequently crossed to Africa and set up at Carthage the first independent German state on Roman soil. In the Battle of the Catalaunian Plains (451), the Roman commander Aëtius, with German support, defeated Attila, who had united his Huns with some other Germans in a vigorous westward push. The Balkans suffered a third period of terrible raids from the eastern Germans; and Jutes, Angles, and Saxons from the Jutland Peninsula crossed over to Britain. The Franks and the Alemanni finally established themselves on the far side of the Rhine, the Burgundians extended along the Rhône valley, and the Visigoths took possession of nearly all of Spain.

In 476 the Germanic soldiery proclaimed Odoacer, a barbarian general, as king of Italy, and, when Odoacer deposed the emperor Romulus Augustulus at Ravenna, the empire in the West was at an end. In the East, imperial rule remained a reality, and Constantinople, also called "New Rome," survived many sieges until its fall in 1453. In comparison, "Old Rome" declined into an episcopal centre, losing many of its imperial characteristics.

RESHAPING THE EMPIRE

By the end of the 5th century, however, most of the non-Roman peoples settled in the West were adopting

Arianism

Arianism is the position that Jesus, as the Son of God, was created by God. It was proposed early in the 4th century by the Alexandrian presbyter Arius and was popular throughout much of the Eastern and Western Roman empires, but inspired major controversy among Christians.

The Council of Nicaea, called by the emperor Constantine in 325, condemned Arius as a heretic and issued a creed to safeguard "orthodox" Christian belief. The creed adopted at Nicaea states that the Son is *homoousion tō Patri* ("of one substance with the Father"), thus declaring him to be all that the Father is: he is completely divine. In fact, however, this was only the beginning of a long dispute.

From 325 to 337, when Constantine died, those church leaders who had supported Arius and had been exiled after the Council of Nicaea attempted to return to their churches and sees (ecclesiastical seats) and banish their enemies. They were partly successful. From 337 to 350 Constans, sympathetic to non-Arian Christians, was emperor in the West, and Constantius II, sympathetic to the Arians, was emperor in the East. In 350 Constantius became sole ruler of the empire, and under his leadership the Nicene party was largely crushed. Constantius eventually transferred his support to the homoeans, led by Acacius, who affirmed that the Son was "like" (*homoios*) the Father.

After Constantius's death (361), the non-Arian Christian majority in the West largely consolidated its position. The persecution of non-Arian Christians conducted by the Arian emperor Valens (364–378) in the East and the success of the teaching of Basil the Great of Caesarea, Gregory of Nyssa, and Gregory of Nazianzus led the homoiousian majority in the East to a fundamental agreement with the Nicene party. When the emperors Gratian (367–383) and Theodosius I (379–395) took up the defense of non-Arian theology, Arianism collapsed. In 381 the second ecumenical council met at Constantinople. Arianism was proscribed, and a statement of faith, the Nicene Creed, was approved. That did not, however, end Arianism as a viable force in the empire. It maintained favor among some groups, most notably some of the Germanic tribes, to the end of the 7th century.

Roman customs and Christian belief. Intermarriage with established Roman families, the assumption of imperial titles, and, finally, conversion assisted a process of acculturation among their leaders, for instance, in the case of Clovis, the Frank. Theodoric the Ostrogoth established an impressive "sub-Roman" kingdom based on Ravenna, where public buildings and churches served by an Arian clergy competed with imperial monuments. Increased Roman influence can also be seen in the law codes proclaimed by the Visigoths Euric (late 5th century) and Alaric II (the Breviary of 506) and the Burgundians, Bavarians, Ostrogoths, and Franks (Lex Salica, 507–511). Christianity often provided the medium for incorporation into old imperial structures. While the Goths were still in the Danube basin, they had embraced Arian Christianity (which denied that the Son was of the same substance as the Father), and their first bishop, Ulfilas, translated the Bible into Gothic. Given its heretical nature, this religious literature in a written vernacular could not survive, and, with conversion to orthodox ("catholic") Christianity, the barbarian languages gradually gave way to Latin.

Nonetheless, the Germanic tribes brought into Europe their own tribal institutions, ethnic patterns, and oral and artistic traditions, including a highly developed epic poetry.

Justinian I, Byzantine emperor from 527 to 565, was noted for his administrative reorganization of the imperial government and for his sponsorship of a codification of laws known as the *Codex Justinianus*.

Their influence was strongest in central Europe, where the Romans had had the least impact; less marked in the northern and eastern parts, where Romano-British and Gallo-Roman cultures were established; and weakest in the highly Romanized southern regions. Linguistically, Old High German developed in the first zone and Anglo-Saxon in Britain, while farther south medieval Romance languages developed from their common Latin inheritance.

In the southern zone, imperial traditions were reinforced by the reconquest, albeit brief, of North Africa, Italy, and parts of Spain by forces from Constantinople under Justinian's general Belisarius. Despite the restoration of Roman administration between 533 and 554 (celebrated in the mosaics of Ravenna and the Pragmatic Sanction of 554), imperial forces could not prevent the Lombards from moving relentlessly into northern Italy, which they occupied in 568. The reconquered parts of the Western Empire were thus reduced to a narrow strip of territory from the head of the Adriatic to Ravenna, Rome—now governed effectively by its bishop—and additional small duchies. In addition, Sicily, Bruttium, and Calabria remained subject to Constantinople and were Greek-speaking for many centuries.

In contrast to previous invaders, from the 6th century onward, newly arrived barbarian forces clung to their pagan culture and resisted assimilation. The Saxons established themselves east of the Rhine in the north. The Avars and their Slav allies, who moved steadily westward from the Vistula and Dnepr river basins, disrupted weak imperial defenses at the Danube and pressed south and west into the Balkans and central Europe. By 567 the Avars established control over the Hungarian plain, where they remained until their

Empress Theodora, shown here with her retinue, was the most trusted adviser of her husband, Justinian I, and probably the most powerful woman in Byzantine history.

defeat by Charlemagne in 796. After successfully besieging Sirmium and Singidunum in the 580s, the eastern Slavs infiltrated the Balkans, while others moved north and west to settle eventually along the Elbe beside the Saxons. The failure of the combined Avaro-Slav siege of Constantinople in 626 ended this pagan expansion. Although Slavs occupied the Balkan Peninsula for two centuries or more, disrupting east-west communication along the ancient Via Egnatia, they were eventually evangelized and absorbed into the Eastern Empire.

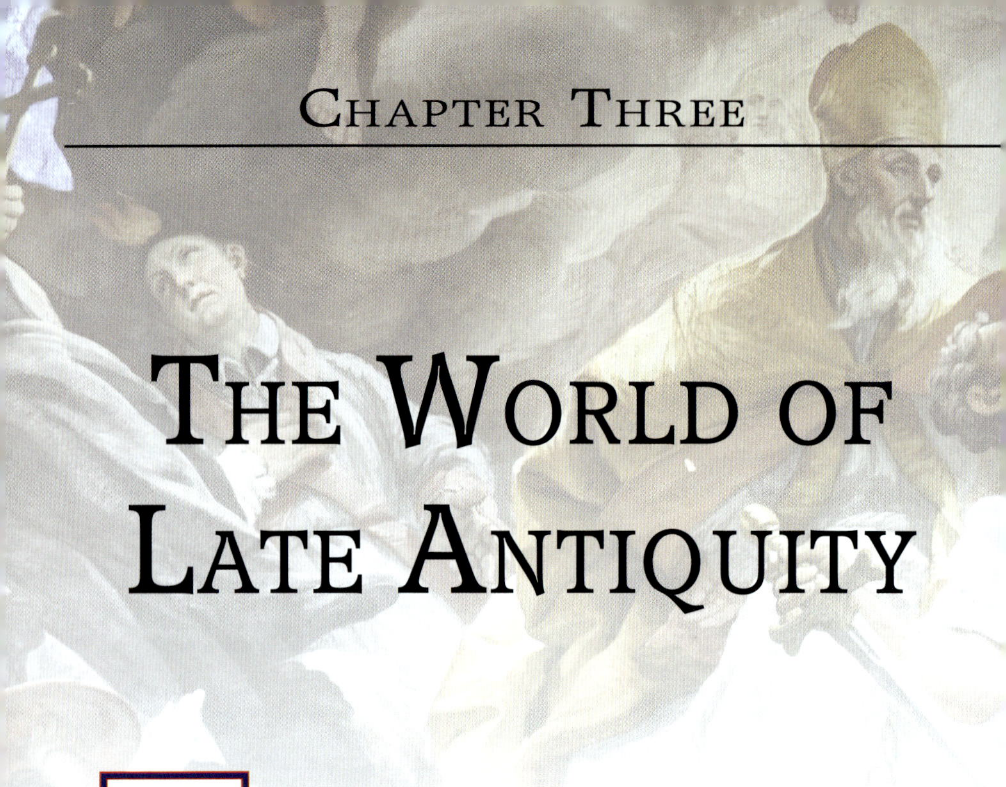

Chapter Three

The World of Late Antiquity

The Roman Empire of late antiquity was no longer the original empire of its founder, Augustus, nor was it even the 2nd-century entity of the emperor Marcus Aurelius. In the 3rd century the emperor, who was first called *princeps* ("first citizen") and then *dominus* ("lord"), became *divus* ("divine"). The powerful religious connotations of the imperial office were adopted even by usurpers of the imperial throne, backed by their armies, who then ruled autocratically at the head of a vast bureaucratic and military organization. Internal and external crises during the 3rd and 4th centuries resulted in the division of the empire into an eastern and a western part after 285, with the east possessing a great and flourishing capital built by the emperor Constantine—Constantinople (now Istanbul)—and far more economic, political, and military resources than the western half. The administration of the entire empire was restructured to finance immense military expenditures, giving the western European provinces and frontier areas greater importance but fewer resources.

THE PEOPLE OF THE EMPIRE

Most of the population of the empire, including soldiers, were frozen hereditarily in their occupations. The Western Empire, whose capital moved north from Rome in the 4th century to a number of provincial cities—Trier, Arles, Milan, and ultimately Ravenna—became less urbanized, more ruralized, and gradually dominated by an aristocracy of landowners and military officials, most of whom lived on large villas and in newly fortified cities. The provincial economy had become increasingly rural and localized and was dominated by the needs of the vast military bases near the frontiers.

The great and small estates were worked by slaves, freedmen, and *coloni* ("farmers"), who had once been independent but had voluntarily or involuntarily subordinated themselves to the great landowners as their only protection against imperial tax collectors or military conscription. The landowners dispensed local justice and assembled private armies, which were powerful enough to negotiate on their subordinates' behalf with imperial officials. Mediterranean trade diminished, and the production of more and more goods was undertaken locally, as was the organization of social, devotional, and political life.

Non-Roman peoples from beyond the frontiers—*barbari* ("barbarians") or *externae gentes* ("foreign peoples"), as the Romans called them—had long been allowed to enter the empire individually or in families as provincial farmers

This mosaic floor is among the remains of a Roman provincial villa at Rockbourne, in present-day Hampshire, England, that dates from the 2nd to 4th century.

and soldiers. But after 375 a number of composite Germanic peoples, many of them only recently assembled and ruled by their own new political and military elites, entered the

empire as intact groups, originally by treaty with Rome and later independently. They established themselves as rulers of a number of western provinces, particularly parts of Italy, Iberia, Gaul, and Britain, often in the name of the Roman emperor and with the cooperation of many Roman provincials.

Roman ethnography classified external peoples as distinct and ethnically homogeneous groups with unchanging identities; they were part of the order of nature. Adopting this view, philologists, anthropologists, and historians in the 19th century maintained that the Germanic "tribes" that first appeared in the 3rd century were the ethnic ancestors of the "tribes" of the 5th century and that the ethnic composition of these groups remained unchanged in the interval. Late 20th-century research thoroughly demonstrated the unreliability of Roman ethnography, although modern concepts of ethnicity continue to exploit it for political purposes.

The Organization of Late Imperial Christianity

The quietly mounting pressure against paganism in the 4th century culminated in the decrees of Emperor Theodosius I (reigned 379–395), who made Catholic Christianity the official religion of the empire and who closed many pagan temples. By the end of the 4th century, therefore, Christianity had been transformed from a persecuted sect to the dominant faith of the empire, in the process becoming intertwined with the imperial government.

The link between church and state was expressed in the civil dignity and insignia granted to bishops, who also began to be entrusted with ambassadorial roles. Constantine himself appointed bishops, and he and his successors convened councils of bishops to address important matters of the faith. By 400 the patriarch of Constantinople (to his avowed embarrassment) enjoyed precedence at court before all civil officials. The emperors issued a number of rulings that afforded greater privilege and responsibility to the bishops, enhancing their position in both church and society. The close relations between the empire and the church in the 4th century were reflected in the writings of Ambrose (bishop of Milan, 374–397), who used "Roman" and "Christian" almost as synonyms. After Theodosius ordered the massacre of the citizens of Thessalonica, however, Ambrose demanded that the emperor undergo penance, thereby enforcing upon Theodosius submission to the church as its son, not its master.

Many Roman provincials were Christian higher clergy. Between the legalization of Christianity by Constantine about 313 and the adoption of Christianity as the legal religion of

Theodosius I is shown here in a detail from an embossed and engraved silver disk, dated to the late 4th century, in the Real Academia de la Historia, Madrid.

Rome by the emperor Theodosius I in 380, Christian communities received immense donations of land, labor, and other gifts from emperors and wealthy converts. The Christian clergy, originally a body of community elders and managerial functionaries, gradually acquired sacramental authority and became aligned with the grades of the imperial civil service. Each *civitas* (community or city), an urban unit and its surrounding district, had its bishop (from the Latin *episcopus*, "overseer"). Because there had been more Roman *civitates* in the Italian and provincial European areas, there were more and usually smaller dioceses in these regions than in the distant north and east.

During the 5th and 6th centuries, bishops gradually assumed greater responsibility for supplying the cities and administering their affairs, replacing the local governments that for centuries had underpinned and constituted the local administration of the empire. Two bishops, Ambrose of Milan (339–397) and Gregory I of Rome (pope 590–604), wrote influential guidebooks on episcopal and other clerical duties and responsibilities toward congregations. These works set standards for all later bishops and are still observed in many churches.

Monasticism

Besides the bishops and their subordinates the priests, who tended to the spiritual and material needs of Christians living in the world—the "secular clergy"—there also existed communities of monks and religious women who had fled the world. These communities were independent, although nominally under the control of the local bishop, and they

Constantine the Great initiated the evolution of the empire into a Christian state and provided the impulse for a Christian culture that prepared the way for the growth of medieval culture.

Benedict of Nursia

Although honored as the "father of western monasticism," Benedict founded no monastic orders. But his rule for governing monastic life

Benedict of Nursia founded the Benedictine monastery at Monte Cassino and is considered the father of Western monasticism.

came to be adopted by ever larger numbers of monasteries in Europe after the 7th century. His rule was a kind of constitution that provided complete guidance for the government of a monastery in its spiritual and material well-being. The rule promoted the ideals of moderation and cooperation in the religious community, and it demanded poverty, obedience, chastity, and fidelity from those who chose the religious life.

The earliest authoritative account of Benedict's life is found in the *Dialogues* of Pope Gregory I, who was pope from 590 to 604. It was written more than 40 years after Benedict's death. Gregory obtained most of his information for *Dialogues* from four of Benedict's disciples. The evidence indicates that Benedict was born at Nursia, Italy, in about 480; that he studied in Rome, where he came under the influence of monastic orders from the Byzantine Empire; and that he turned to monasticism as a way of getting away from the evils of Rome.

He retired to Subiaco, 40 miles (65 kilometers) east of Rome, and lived in a cave there for several years. When his reputation as a holy man spread, disciples came to him and pleaded with him to found a monastery. His reforming efforts were resisted, however, and an attempt was made to poison him. He returned to his cave, but disciples continued to flock to him.

He founded 12 monasteries in the vicinity of Subiaco and after a few years started the great abbey at Monte Cassino, south of Rome. Benedict's sister, Scholastica, lived near Monte Cassino as head of a nunnery. When Benedict died, he was buried in the abbey's Oratory of St. John the Baptist.

St. Benedict's death was recorded by monks on March 21, which became the traditional day of his death.

followed diverse rules of life—hence their designation as "regular clergy" (from *regula*, "rule"). The most influential monastic rule in Latin Christianity after the 8th century was that of Benedict of Nursia (*c.* 480–*c.* 547). Benedict's rule provided for a monastic day of work, prayer, and contemplation, offering psychological balance in the monk's life. It also elevated the dignity of manual labour in the service of God, long scorned by the elites of antiquity. Benedict's monastery at Monte Cassino, south of Rome, became one of the greatest centres of Benedictine monasticism.

Benedict's Rule is notable for its humanity and its balance of prayer and work. Because the manual work of monks often consisted of the copying of manuscripts, the monasteries became a great centre of cultural life for centuries. For example, Benedict's contemporary Cassiodorus (c. 490–c. 585) had the works of classical authors (such as Cicero and Quintilian) copied, as well as Hebrew Scriptures, the New Testament, and the works of the early Church Fathers.

The word "monasticism" is derived from the Greek *monachos* ("living alone"), but this etymology highlights only one of the elements of monasticism and is somewhat misleading, because a large proportion of the world's monastics live in cenobitic (common life) communities. The term "monasticism" implies celibacy, or living alone in the sense of lacking a spouse, which became a socially and historically crucial feature of the monastic life.

Paul of Thebes (*right*) and his disciple St. Anthony are depicted in this image displayed at the Coptic Museum in Cairo, Egypt.

A more appropriate word for early Christian monasticism, as well as for that practiced by Eastern religions today, might be "asceticism." It means self-denial, and it is rooted in a negative attitude toward the world. In Christianity the ascetics looked upon the world as a source of temptation and sin. By secluding themselves from it, monks hoped to avoid harmful contacts and to concentrate their energies upon salvation alone.

The earliest Christian hermits of the Egyptian desert (c. 250–500 ce), known as the "Desert Fathers"—Anthony of Egypt, Paul of Thebes, Pachomius of the Thebaid, and others—presaged later monastic institutions. The early hermits, mostly native Egyptian peasants, were inspired by the example of famous recluses and by biblical exemplars such as Elijah and Jesus (during his 40 days in the wilderness). However, their rigorous asceticism generated an impulse toward cenobitism (literally "lying [i.e., eating, sleeping, living] together") and a life based on military models, which appear in virtually all monastic traditions. The community was viewed as composed of soldiers of the spirit, who were combatting the forces of evil by facing the temptations of the Devil in the desert.

The first of the Christian monks was St. Anthony (251–356). Communal, or cenobitic, monasticism was first organized by St. Pachomius (c. 290–346), who also composed the first monastic rule. Basil, bishop of Caesarea Cappadociae (370–379), rejected the solitary ideal, insisting on communities with a rule safeguarding the bishop's authority and with concrete acts of service to perform (e.g., hospital work and teaching). Early Christian monasticism spread beyond Egypt and assumed different forms, most famously

This 5th-century Christian funerary relief depicts St. Simeon Stylites and the pillar he lived on.

in the example of the Syrian ascetic Simeon Stylites (c. 390–459), who lived for nearly 40 years atop a pillar that was said to measure just three feet (one metre) across.

While the earliest examples of Christian monasticism were a response to contemporary social conditions, the practice had scriptural roots and reflected the attraction of the ascetic life that had long been part of the Christian and philosophical traditions. The ascetic practices of Egyptian and Syrian monks were transplanted to western Europe through texts such as the 4th-century Latin translation of the *Life of Saint Antony* (by Patriarch Athanasius of Alexandria) and through widely traveled observers such as the theologian and monk John Cassian (360–435). These Mediterranean-wide influences were among the last examples of the communications network of the older, ecumenical Mediterranean world. Monasticism developed and sustained a powerful ascetic dimension in both Greek and Latin Christianity that increased in importance as monasticism itself came to define the ideal of clerical life in the West.

In the case of Martin (316–397), a former Roman soldier turned wandering holy man, monastic asceticism was combined with the office episcopal, as Martin eventually became bishop of Tours in Gaul. He emphasized the conversion of rural pagans, as well as ministering to the urban and rural elites. In the Iberian Peninsula the work of the monk and bishop Martin of Braga (c. 515–580) was also devoted to the religious instruction of rustics. His work provided an influential model for the later conversion of northern and eastern Europe.

This altar panel shows the legend of St. Martin of Tours dividing his cloak to share with a beggar. Martin was the first great leader of Western monasticism.

Heterodoxy and Heresy

While Greek Christians called their church and religion Orthodox, Latin Christians adopted the term Catholic (from *catholicus*, "universal"). The term "catholic Christianity" was originally used to authenticate a normative, orthodox Christian cult (system of religious belief and ritual) on the grounds of its universality and to characterize different beliefs and practices as heterodox on the grounds that they were merely local and did not reflect duration, unanimity, or universality. These three characteristics of Latin orthodoxy were defined by the 5th-century monastic writer Vincent of Lérins (died *c.* 450) and adopted generally throughout the Latin church.

Devotional movements that differed from the norms of orthodoxy were defined as heterodoxy, or heresy. The earliest of these were several forms of Judaizing Christianity and Gnosticism, a dualist belief in asceticism and spiritual enlightenment. Once Christianity was established throughout the empire, other local movements were also condemned. Donatism, the belief among many North African Christians that Christian leaders who had bowed to pagan imperial persecution before 313 had lost their priestly status and needed to be reordained, was the first major heterodox practice to be considered—and condemned—at an imperial church council (411). Other movements were Arianism, which challenged the divinity of Jesus, and Pelagianism, which denied original sin and emphasized purely human abilities to achieve salvation. Other beliefs, usually those that contradicted increasingly normative doctrines of Trinitarianism (the belief that the Godhead includes three coequal, coeternal, and consubstantial persons)

St. Athanasius was the chief defender of Christian orthodoxy in the 4th-century battle against Arianism.

or Christology (the interpretation of the nature of Christ), were also condemned as heresy.

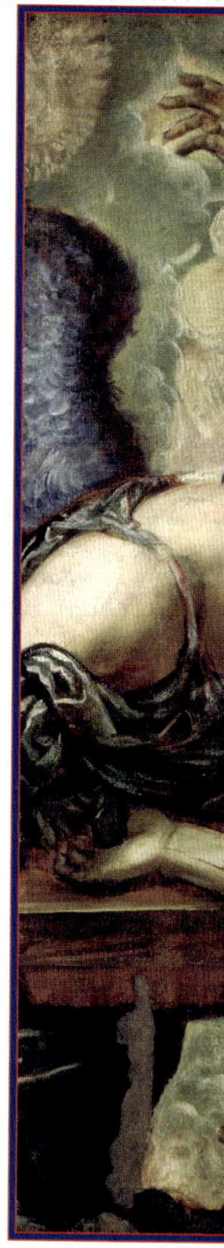

Trinitarianism and Christology

The doctrine of Trinitarianism—the unity of Father, Son, and Holy Spirit as three persons in one Godhead—developed gradually over several centuries and through many controversies. Neither the word "Trinity" nor the explicit doctrine appears in the New Testament. Initially, both the requirements of monotheism inherited from the Hebrew Scriptures and the need to interpret the biblical teaching to Greco-Roman religions seemed to demand that the divine in Christ as the Word, or Logos, be interpreted as subordinate to the Supreme Being. An alternative solution was to interpret Father, Son, and Holy Spirit as three modes of the self-disclosure of the one God but not as distinct within the being of God itself. The first tendency recognized the distinctness among the three, but at the cost of their equality and their unity. The second came to terms with their unity, but at the cost of their distinctness as "persons."

It was not until the 4th century that the distinctness of the three and their unity were brought together in a single orthodox doctrine of one essence and three persons. The Council of Nicaea in 325 stated the crucial formula for that doctrine in its confession that the Son is "of the same substance [*homoousios*] as the Father," even though it said very little about the Holy Spirit. Over the next half

The Trinity (1564) is an oil on canvas painting by Tintoretto; it hangs in the Galleria Sabauda in Turin, Italy.

century, Athanasius defended and refined the Nicene formula, and, by the end of the 4th century, under the leadership of Basil of Caesarea, Gregory of Nyssa, and Gregory of Nazianzus (the Cappadocian Fathers), the doctrine of the Trinity took substantially the form it has maintained ever since.

Christology is the part of theology that is concerned with the nature and work of Jesus, including such matters as the Incarnation, the Resurrection, and his human and divine natures and their relationship. Reflections about Jesus dominated Christian discourse from the apostolic age onward. Most of that Christological reflection took place in the eastern Mediterranean, where it utilized the language (Greek) and concepts of Classical antiquity. Since there seem to be echoes of Classical concepts in Scripture, it is not surprising that Christian theologians appropriated them in order to explicate the meaning of Christian affirmations. Two notions in particular played important roles: logos theology and preexistence.

Logos theology, which was formulated by the Jewish philosopher Philo, aimed to describe how God is active and effective through the divine will, reason, and power. That activity was named the *logos* (Greek: "word") of God. Christian reflection understood Jesus as the manifestation of the divine will, reason, and power and therefore applied the concept of the logos to him.

That concept of preexistence held that everything good on earth was preexistent with God, existing in God's cognition. The good thus existed with God before any earthly appearance, which is merely the transition from hiding to manifestation. The concept of preexistence is related to the notion that there is nothing that God does not know, that there is neither past nor future with God, and that God is the Lord of History.

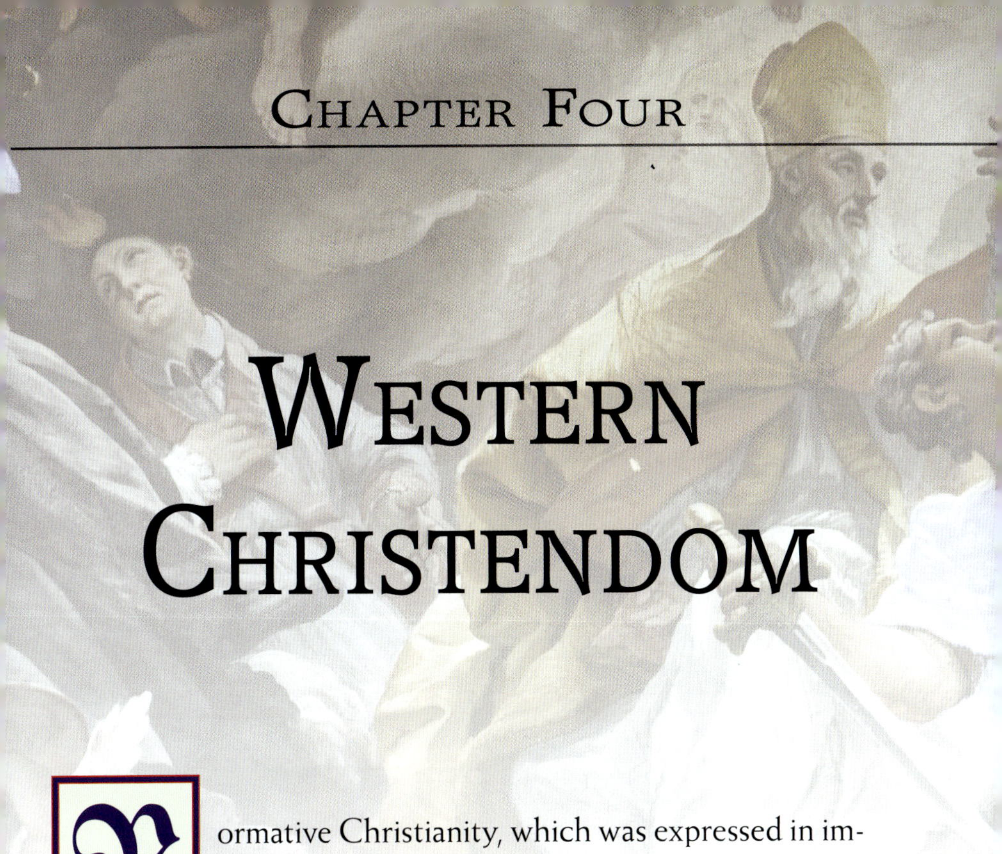

Chapter Four

Western Christendom

Normative Christianity, which was expressed in imperial legislation, church councils, and the works of influential Christian writers, gradually became the faith of Europe's new regional rulers. Within that broad, universal ideology, however, many of the new kings and peoples based their claims to legitimacy and a common identity on their own versions of Latin Christianity, as expressed in local law, ritual, saints' cults, sacred spaces and shrines, and saints' relics. Relics are, strictly speaking, the mortal remains of a saint. But in the broad sense, the term also includes any object that has been in contact with the saint. The basis of Christian cult veneration of relics is the idea that reverence for the relics rebounds to the honour of the saint. The cults of saints and their relics served to territorialize devotion, and control over them was a distinctive sign of legitimate power. Although the older empire and the new, nonimperial lands

St. Helena, the mother of Constantine the Great, was said to have discovered the True Cross, the cross upon which Jesus was crucified, in the 4th century.

in Europe into which a new culture expanded came to call themselves Christianitas ("Christendom"), they were in practice divided into many self-contained entities that have been called "micro-Christendoms," each based on the devotional identity of king, clerics, and people.

Kings and Peoples

The kings of new peoples ruled as much in Roman style as they could, issuing laws written in Latin for their own peoples and their Roman subjects and striking coins that imitated imperial coinage. They also sponsored the composition of "ethnic" and genealogical histories that attributed to themselves and their peoples, however recently assembled, an identity and antiquity rivaling that of Rome. Although the Romans, who called their own society a *populus* ("civil people"), used the term *rex* ("king") only for rulers of peoples at lower levels of sociocultural development, the political order of kings and peoples became a commonplace in Europe in late antiquity and would remain so until the 19th century. Some of these kingdoms, especially that of the Visigoths in southern Gaul and later in Iberia, also modeled themselves on the ancient Hebrew kingdoms as described in Scripture. They borrowed and adapted some ancient Jewish rituals, such as liturgically anointing the ruler with oil and reminding him in sermons, prayers, and meetings of church councils that he was God's servant, with spiritual and political responsibilities that legitimized his power.

As the cultures associated with the new kings and peoples spread throughout western Europe from the 5th to the 8th centuries, they influenced political and religious change

This image from a 15th-century manuscript depicts the finding of the Holy Cross.

in areas that the empire had never ruled—initially Ireland, then northern Britain, the lower Rhineland, and trans-Rhenish Europe (the lands east of the Rhine River). The bishop and the monk were two of the most remarkable and longest enduring religious and social inventions of late antiquity; the barbarian kingdoms were a third. Although many of the latter did not survive, their experiments in Christian kingship, as represented in texts, ritual, pictures, and objects, began a long tradition in European political life and thought.

The Great Commission

The process of expansion was also driven by a missionary mandate rooted in the New Testament itself. Matthew 28:19–20 says "Go therefore and make disciples of all nations, baptizing them in the name of the Father and of the Son and of the Holy Spirit, teaching them to observe all that I have commanded you; and lo, I am with you always, to the close of the age," while Mark 16:15 commands "Go into all the world and proclaim the good news to the whole creation."

Reflecting a new, literal, and personal understanding of Jesus' command in the Gospels to baptize and to proclaim the word of God, the work of conversion to Christianity was extended to all peoples, not just to those of the empire. Conversion was carried out at first by individual Christians acting on their own, not as agents of an organized church. Greek Christians from Constantinople also undertook missionary work, sometimes individually but also as an increasingly prominent aspect of Byzantine imperial diplomacy in the Balkans and north of the Danube valley and the Black Sea. In the eastern parts of the Byzantine Empire, communities

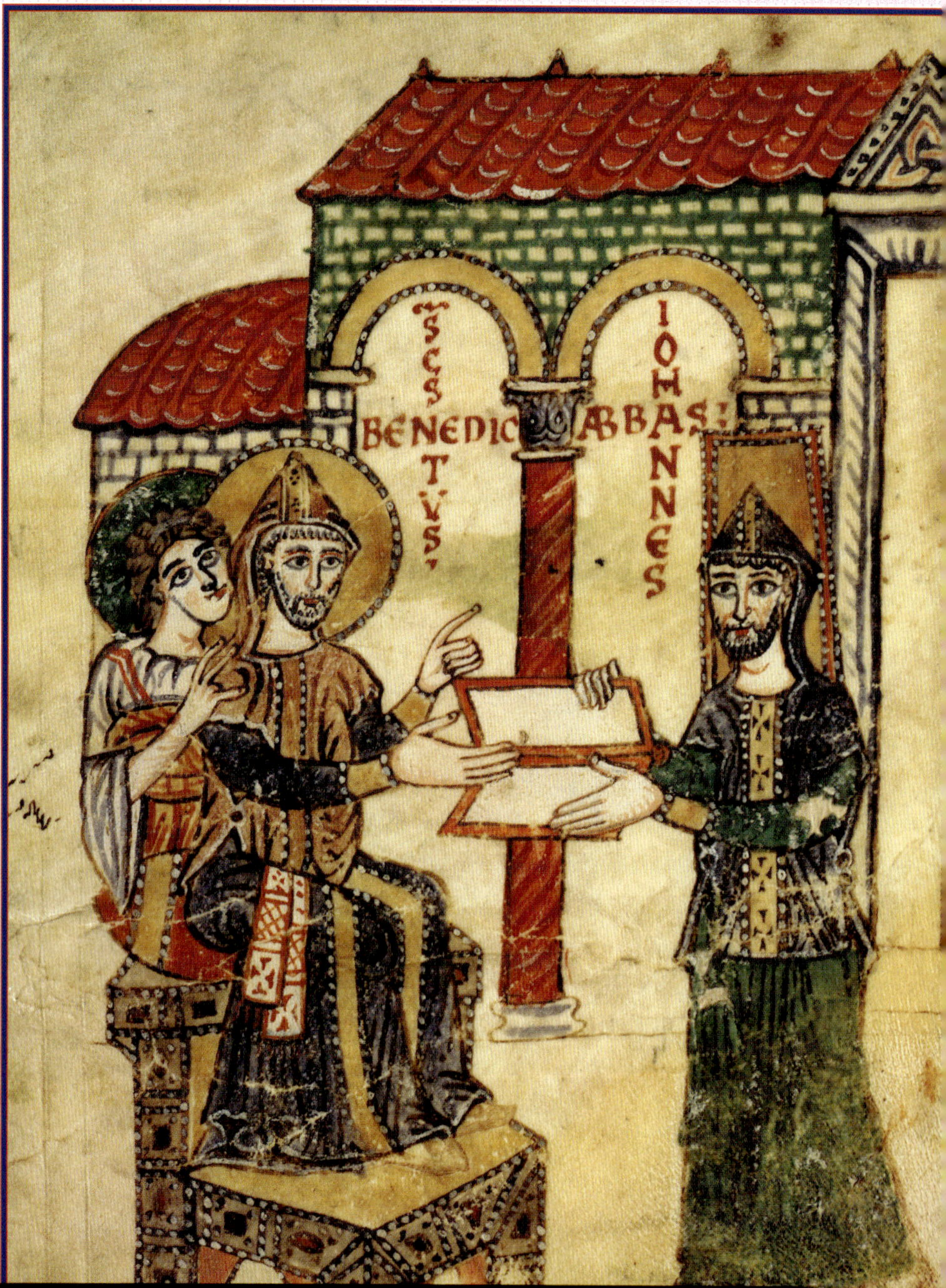

This illustration from a 10th-century manuscript depicts abbots John and St. Benedict.

of Nestorian Christians, who stressed the independence of the human and divine persons of Christ, moved beyond the imperial frontiers, first into Persia and then farther east. By the 10th century a long string of such settlements ran along the Silk Road from the Mediterranean to China.

Individual conversion stories were modeled on that of St. Paul the Apostle (Acts of the Apostles 9–10), which itself was echoed in the *Confessions* of St. Augustine. Individual conversion experiences touched people in all walks of life: Martin of Tours, the soldier turned ascetic and bishop; the Gallo-Roman aristocrats Sulpicius Severus—who wrote the influential life of Martin—and Caesarius of Arles; and the free Romano-Briton St. Patrick, who had been a slave in pagan Ireland and returned to convert his former captors.

But the most widely accepted model of conversion of both religious belief and practice was collective—that of a ruler and his followers together as a new Christian people. In this way, the king and church integrated rulership with clerical teaching and the development of the liturgy and with the definition of sacred space, control of sanctity, and the rituals surrounding key moments in human life, from baptism to death and burial. Along with the conversion of the Visigoths from Arian to Catholic Christianity, two of the most notable collective conversions were those of the Frankish leader Clovis and the English king Ethelbert of Kent.

Clovis was married to a Christian, Clotilda of Burgundy (later St. Clotilda), but reportedly remained indifferent to religion until two incidents changed his mind. First, the couple's infant son was cured of an illness. Then, in 496, Clovis's army, near defeat in a campaign against the invading Alemanni, won a sudden and decisive victory. Convinced

St. Patrick (*right*), the patron saint and national apostle of Ireland, is credited with bringing Christianity to Ireland.

that these favorable events were evidence of the power of Christ, Clovis sought to be converted. Along with his leading warrior chiefs, he was subsequently baptized by Remigius at Reims. Recent research, however, has complicated the traditional account. It suggests that Clovis may have expressed an interest in Arianism (perhaps even converting to it prior to his conversion to Catholicism) and was actually baptized rather late in life, possibly at Christmas in 508, only three years before his death.

Known as the Apostle of the English, Augustine of Canterbury was responsible for the conversion of millions of people to Christianity. Augustine was prior of the Benedictine monastery of St. Andrew in Rome when Pope Gregory I chose him to lead a missionary group of 40 monks going to England. The entourage arrived in the spring of 597 and was well received by King Ethelbert I, whose wife was already a Christian. Ethelbert was soon baptized, which encouraged many of his subjects to be converted. Reportedly thousands were baptized on Christmas Day 597. Augustine sent a report of his remarkable progress to the pope, and Gregory responded by dispatching more missionaries to help with the work. Augustine was consecrated bishop of the English church in the fall of 597 and made his headquarters at Canterbury in a church provided by the king. During the next 90 years most of England was converted by his followers. His only failure to win converts was in Wales, where Christianity antedated his arrival. These churches refused to accept the authority of the pope in Rome and would not cooperate with Augustine in unification with the churches he was founding.

In this 19th-century coloured wood engraving, St. Augustine preaches to Ethelbert I.

THE IRISH AND ENGLISH INFLUENCE

As Romans and non-Romans locally assimilated into new peoples during the 6th and 7th centuries, non-Romans, as had Romans before them, became Christian monks, higher clergy, and sometimes saints. In the late 5th century the conversion of Ireland, the first Christianized territory that had never been part of the Roman Empire, brought the particularly Irish ascetic practice of self-exile to bear on missionary work. In the 6th century the Irish monk Columba (c. 521–597) exiled himself to the island of Iona, from which he began to convert the peoples of southwestern Scotland. Other Irish monk-exiles moved through the Rhine valley, Austria, Bavaria, Switzerland, and northern Italy. Columban (c. 543–615), the most influential of these missionaries, greatly reformed the devotional life of the Frankish nobility and founded monasteries at Sankt Gallen, Luxeuil, and Bobbio. Irish and Scottish devotional practices also influenced England, where Celtic forms of Christianity clashed with Continental, especially Roman, forms—a conflict resolved at the Synod of Whitby in 664, when Roman norms were adopted first for the kingdom of Northumbria and later for other English kingdoms. Irish influence remained strong in the English church, however, especially in matters of learning, church reform, missionary exile, and clerical organization.

From the late 7th century, English pilgrims visited Rome, creating a strong devotional link between Rome and Britain, which was reasserted wherever English missionary activity took place. Benedict Biscop, an English noble, traveled to Rome several times, returning with Roman books and pictures. He founded the twin monasteries of Wearmouth and Jarrow (the saintly scholar Bede was a monk of Wearmouth-Jarrow) and escorted the learned Theodore of Tarsus back to England when Theodore was appointed archbishop of Canterbury. Theodore's pastoral and educational activities greatly enhanced English clerical culture, producing both a network of schools and a missionary consciousness that sent English monks, like their Irish predecessors, to the Continent.

The most influential of these figures was Boniface (c. 675–754), the first archbishop of Mainz, who spent much of his adult life in missionary and reform work in and around the edges of the kingdom of the Franks. The letters of Boniface demonstrate his respect for Rome and provide important information about his missionary activities. His great monastery of Fulda played an important role in both reform and conversion. The abbey became a missionary centre, and its school was one of Europe's important seats of learning during the early Middle Ages, after Rabanus Maurus became its director in 803. It employed 12 manuscript copyists, and its great library survived until the 17th century.

THE BISHOPS OF ROME

Throughout their history, the bishops of Rome enjoyed great respect and veneration because of the antiquity of their see, its historical orthodoxy, the relics of its martyrs (including Saints Peter and Paul the Apostles), and the

This stained-glass window in a chapel at Edinburgh Castle in Edinburgh, Scotland, depicts Saint Columba.

The Venerable Bede

Bede (also spelled Beda or Baeda) (673?–735) was an English Roman Catholic saint, called the Father of English History. He established the practice of dating events from the birth of Christ by using the designation AD, or *anno Domini* (in the year of the Lord). His most famous work, *Historia Ecclesiastica Gentis Anglorum* (*Ecclesiastical History of the English People*), which he finished in 731, is a primary source of information on the early history of the church and of England, particularly on the conversion of the Anglo-Saxon tribes. The work covers British history from about 55 BCE to 600 CE and is noted for its painstaking separation of historical fact from hearsay and its documentation of sources. He was one of the best-educated men of his time and had a major influence on English literature as well as on the church.

Bede was born in what is now Northumberland and at the age of seven was sent to the monastery of St. Peter in Wearmouth to be educated by the abbot Benedict Biscop. He was later sent to the nearby monastery of St. Paul in Jarrow, where he studied under the abbot Ceolfrith. Bede was ordained a deacon in 692, at an age that was much younger than usual, and became a priest when he was only about 30 years old. Other than a few short trips, Bede spent most of his life inside the monastery, devoting his time to studying, writing, teaching, and praying. Besides studying Latin, Greek, and classical writings and doctrines, he also learned Hebrew, medicine, astronomy, and the science of verse making. He wrote about 40 books, including lives of the saints, hymns, epigrams, works on chronology and grammar, and commentaries on the Old and New Testaments.

Shown in a detail of a manuscript from Fulda Abbey in the 10th to 11th century, St. Boniface baptizes converts into the German Church.

imperial and Christian history of the city of Rome. The material conditions of the 6th and 7th centuries, however, greatly limited any papal exercise of universal authority or influence, and the popes developed relatively little theory about papal authority of any kind over all Christians.

Like other bishops, however, the bishops of Rome benefited from the idea of *traditio* (Latin: "tradition"), which stated that the authority of the Apostles had been passed down to the Christian higher clergy. They also gradually assumed more and more responsibility for the administration of the city itself. Because Rome was Rome and because the properties of the Roman church extended throughout Italy, the papal administration of the city and the invocation of its Christian, rather than imperial, past slowly turned it into the Rome of St. Peter, who accordingly assumed an increasingly important role in medieval spirituality. This Christianized Rome was a place that the diversified societies of western Europe could revere and visit because of its devotional centrality in the Latin Christian world.

Pope Gregory the Great is depicted in a carved ivory book cover, c. 980, in the Kunsthistorisches Museum, Vienna.

Between the 5th and the 11th centuries, many argued that, just as there had been a hierarchy of cities in the old empire, there was a hierarchy of bishops, and the bishop of Rome stood at its head. Although the idea of papal supremacy in Latin Christendom found a number of papal and non-papal exponents during this period, it did not become dominant until the late 11th century. Even before then, however, the affection and respect for Rome built up in England and in the kingdom of the Franks did much to increase the attractiveness of the papacy.

Conclusion

During the 7th and 8th centuries, new invasions of the eastern part of the empire and the emergence of Islam, first in the Arabian Peninsula and then to the west in Egypt and Numidia and to the east in Persia, divided the old Mediterranean ecumenical world into three distinct culture zones: East Rome, or Byzantium; Islam; and Latin Europe. Byzantium and western Europe remained long on the defensive against Islamic pressures, which extended to the conquest of the Iberian Peninsula in 711, Sicily in 902, and Anatolia in the 11th century. Each of these three cultures developed its own character based on different uses of and attitudes toward the Roman-Mediterranean ecumenical past. They maintained diplomatic and commercial contact with each other, though sometimes on a much-reduced scale, and continued to influence each other culturally even as they became more distinct. In spite of their increasing distinctiveness, they were never entirely separated, since both trade and the transmission of ideas passed through their porous edges. In addition, large numbers of Jews and Christians continued to live as privileged religious aliens in most of the Muslim world.

Despite the division of the Mediterranean world into these three culture zones, Christianity's influence widened even more when the great Charlemagne of the Carolingian dynasty became king of the Franks in 768. He brought the Lombards and pagan Saxons under his sway. Charlemagne was a great conqueror who sought to spread the faith as he expanded his kingdom throughout much of western Europe. He supported missionaries and strove to improve the religious life in his realm. He also worked to defend the church with his great army and to protect the pope from enemies in Italy. In 800 the pope crowned Charlemagne emperor to strengthen ties between pope and king.

Glossary

AESTHETIC Relating to sensuous cognition.

APOSTOLIC Of or relating to a succession of spiritual authority from the apostles held (as by Roman Catholics, Anglicans, and Eastern Orthodox) to be perpetuated by successive ordinations of bishops and to be necessary for valid sacraments and orders.

ARIANISM A theological movement initiated by Arius that held that Jesus, as the son of God, was created by God. It won strong support during the 4th century BCE chiefly in the Eastern churches, but it was condemned in general councils at Nicaea (325 CE) and Constantinople (381 CE).

ASCETICISM Rigorous abstention from self-indulgence.

BARBARIAN Of or relating to a land, culture, or people alien and usually believed to be inferior to one's own.

CENOBITIC Related to a religious group that lives together in common.

CLERICAL Of, relating to, or characteristic of the clergy, the body of men and women duly ordained to the service of God in the Christian church.

CONFESSIONAL Adhering to, established on, or defined by a confession of faith.

DEVOTIONAL Related to earnestness and zeal in the performance of religious duties and observations.

ECCLESIASTICAL Of or relating to a church, especially as a formal and established institution.

ECUMENICAL Promoting or tending toward worldwide Christian unity.

EPISCOPAL Of, being, or suited to a bishop.

ETHNOGRAPHY A branch of anthropology that deals historically with the origin and filiation of societies and cultures.

EVANGELIZE To instruct in the gospel; to convert to Christianity.

FRANK A member of a Germanic-speaking people who invaded the western Roman Empire in the 5th century.

GOTHS A member of a Germanic people that in ancient times dwelt between the Elbe and the Vistula and in the early centuries of the Christian era overran the Roman Empire.

HERESY (HETERODOXY) Adherence to a religious opinion that is contrary to an established dogma of a church.

HUN A member of a nomadic central Asian people who were driven westward from Mongolia about 200 BCE and after obtaining control of a large portion of central and eastern Europe under Attila in about the middle of the 5th century forced even Rome to pay tribute until their power was terminated by their defeat at Châlons in 451 and the death of Attila in 453

LITURGICAL Related to a rite or series of rites, observances, or procedures prescribed for public worship in the Christian church in accordance with authorized or standard form.

MONASTICISM Organized asceticism as practiced in a monastery.

ORTHODOX Conforming to the Christian faith as formulated in the church creeds and confessions.

PHILOLOGICAL Related to literary or classical learning.

PROVINCIAL Of or relating to a province; one living in or coming from a province.

ROMANIZATION The act or process by which an area became Romanized, or brought into the cultures and traditions of Rome.

SUPERIMPOSITION The attachment or coexistence of two entities.

VENERATION A feeling of respect mingled with awe excited by the dignity, wisdom, or superiority of something, by sacredness, by consecrated state, or by hallowed association.

VERNACULAR Using a language or dialect native to a region or country rather than a literary, cultured, or foreign language.

Bibliography

Greeks, Romans, and Barbarians

Appropriate volumes of the multivolume series *Cambridge Ancient History* (1923–2005) survey the development and interaction of the civilizations. Emily Vermeule, *Greece in the Bronze Age* (1964, reprinted 1972), is a standard work on Aegean civilization. Other detailed treatments include Chester G. Starr, *The Origins of Greek Civilization, 1100–650 B.C.* (1961); N.G.L. Hammond, *A History of Greece to 322 B.C.*, 3rd ed. (1986); J.B. Bury and Russell Meiggs, *A History of Greece to the Death of Alexander the Great*, 4th ed. (1975); and Oswyn Murray, *Early Greece* (1980). John Boardman, *The Greek Overseas: Their Early Colonies and Trade*, new ed. (1980), provides an overview of commercial expansion; and Erich S. Gruen, *The Hellenistic World and the Coming of Rome*, 2 vol. (1984), is a history of the Roman conquest of the Hellenistic states.

H.H. Scullard, *A History of the Roman World: 753–146 BC*, 4th ed. (1980), is a standard comprehensive survey. Other relevant histories are Jacques Heurgon, *The Rise of Rome to 264 B.C.* (1973; originally published in French, 1969); Kurt A. Raaflaub (ed.), *Social Struggles in Archaic Rome: New Perspectives on the Conflict of the Orders* (1986), focusing on the social life, customs, and class structure of republican Rome; William V. Harris, *War and Imperialism in Republican Rome, 327–70 B.C.* (1979, reprinted 1985), on Roman expansion; Joseph Vogt, *The Decline of Rome: The Metamorphosis of Ancient Civilization* (1967; originally published in German, 1965); and A.H.M. Jones, *The Later Roman Empire, 284–602: A Social Economic and Administrative Survey*, 2 vol. (1964, reprinted 1986). Michael Grant and

Rachel Kitzinger (eds.), *Civilization of the Ancient Mediterranean: Greece and Rome*, 3 vol. (1988), is a comprehensive collection of essays on cultural, economic, and social life in the Classical world.

André Piganiol, *L'Empire chrétien* (325–395), 2nd ed. updated by André Chastagnol (1972), offers an exceptionally rich and informative narrative among modern works on the later Roman Empire. Diana Bowder, *The Age of Constantine and Julian* (1978), is good on those two reigns. On a major development, monasticism, Derwas J. Chitty, *The Desert a City: An Introduction to the Study of Egyptian and Palestinian Monasticism Under the Christian Empire* (1966, reissued 1977), is highly readable. Ramsay MacMullen, *Corruption and the Decline of Rome* (1988), includes an up-to-date survey of evidence for decline, and also argues a thesis. Herwig Wolfram, *History of the Goths* (1988; originally published in German, 2nd ed., 1980), is a superb study of a crucial player in the 4th to 6th centuries. Walter Goffart, *Barbarians and Romans, A.D. 418–584: The Techniques of Accommodation* (1980), carries the account further.

Brief illustrated surveys of 600 years of post-Classical history are presented in Gerald Simons, *Barbarian Europe* (1968); and Philip Dixon, *Barbarian Europe* (1976). Otto J. Maenchen-Helfen, *The World of the Huns: Studies in Their History and Culture* (1973), offers a scholarly examination of the development of early Europe.

THE MIDDLE AGES

Useful reference works are *The New Cambridge Medieval History*, 7 vol. (1995–2005); *Dictionary of the Middle Ages*, 13 vol.

(1982–89); and *Encyclopedia of the Middle Ages*, 2 vol. (2000). A good outline of events in the Middle Ages is R.L. Storey, *Chronology of the Medieval World, 800–1491* (1973). A discussion of late antiquity is G.W. Bowersock, Peter Brown, and Oleg Grabar (eds.), *Late Antiquity: A Guide to the Postclassical World* (1999).

Surveys (cited here in reverse chronological sequence) include Eamon Duffy, *Saints & Sinners: A History of the Popes*, 3rd ed. (2006); Peter Brown, *The Rise of Western Christendom: Triumph and Diversity AD 200–1000*, 2nd ed. (2003); Rosamond McKitterick (ed.), *The Early Middle Ages: Europe, 400–1000* (2001); R.I. Moore, *The First European Revolution*, c. 970–1215 (2000); and Marcia L. Colish, *Medieval Foundations of the Western Intellectual Tradition, 400–1400* (1998, reprinted 2002).

HISTORIOGRAPHY OF THE MIDDLE AGES

Biographies of some important historians can be found in Helen Damico and Joseph Zavadil (eds.), *Medieval Scholarship: Biographical Studies in the Formation of a Discipline*, 3 vol. (1995–99). Two important volumes that represent scholarly perspectives of the late 20th and early 21st century are Peter Linehan and Janet L. Nelson, *The Medieval World* (2001); and Lester K. Little and Barbara Rosenwein (eds.), *Debating the Middle Ages: Issues and Readings* (1998).

Terminology and periodization are discussed in Fred C. Robinson, "Medieval, the Middle Ages," *Speculum*, 59(4):745–756 (October 1984); William A. Green, "Periodization in European and World History," *Journal of World History*, 3(1):13–53 (Spring 1992); Lionel Gossman,

Medievalism and the Ideologies of the Enlightenment: The World and Work of La Curne de Sainte-Palaye (1968); Jacques Le Goff, "The Several Middle Ages of Jules Michelet," in his *Time, Work, and Culture in the Middle Ages* (1980), pp. 3–28; Timothy Reuter, "Medieval: Another Tyrannous Construct?," *The Medieval History Journal*, 1(1):25–45 (1998), and other articles in the same number.

Index